Welcome Home

This story is a declaration of love for one and all.

I dedicate it to all the healers, teachers, energy workers and
peacemakers of this world.

This is my love letter to all those that have shown me the way home. To all the people that have been courageous enough to fight through the illusion of separateness, and have chosen to heal themselves and the world.

This is the story of my life's progression to become a shepherd of conscious evolution: a guide through the wondrous, but also challenging, process of spiritual ascension; my insights into mastering ancient meditation techniques; and honouring the sacred mystical arts of our ancestors.

We are living in the age of a spectacular evolutionary leap. Human beings have been waking up through a glorious spiritual ascension process. There has been suffering. It has been a tiring, confusing and invigorating trial for us all, but we are stronger for it. There are valuable lessons to be found when facing fear and bearing pain: most importantly, the realisation that we are deeply connected as one; that we are not alone, and never were. A new era has begun: an illuminating force of transcendence to unity consciousness. I like to think of it as Rainbow energy flowing into our world, liberating the people and waking us all up to this precious moment in time to shine.

Three very special women, Kiki Falconer, Agatha Da Rosa, and Rosenbelle Ganan, have helped me reach this pertinent moment, and I am so grateful and excited for the future with you all in my life. Thank you. I honour the rise of the Goddess in all of us.

Introduction

Neil Greenwood is a meditation expert and spiritual healer, currently teaching mindfulness and healing practices worldwide. Deeply fascinated by universal knowledge and human potential, he lives the life of a spiritual scientist, forever learning and advancing his own creative and intellectual acumen.

Along this path, he opened up to divine instruction, activating his highest potential from within, which allowed him to enhance his psychic abilities and communicate with the world of spirit.

Consider what follows to be a guide to uncover the practical application of these areas of interest:

Ancient meditation practices
Lucid dreaming and astral projection
Accessing the realms of the super-conscious
Yogic chakra alignment and awakening the kundalini

Neil is the leader of Echochamber, a community of 'light'-minded individuals, who are awake and involved with the positive transformation taking place in this world here and now. He welcomes you to join this group:

www.facebook.com/groups/echochamberdreams/

Chapter 1

Where to begin?

We are privileged to be living in the Golden Age of human existence. It is clear to see how our behaviour affects one another and our environment. We play an active and critical role in the process of evolution for ourselves and all living beings on our planet. This is the meaning of our great awakening, the time when human beings awaken and acknowledge our respective roles as co-creators. There is no longer a need for borders and separation. We are human beings, different colours, races, genders, but yet one and the same: brothers and sisters of the human race and we know just how powerful we are when we stand together. This will forever be my view of the world around me. It is my message to deliver: hope and revelation.

These past seven years have seen a tremendous change in my life. I had a very normal upbringing, my parents had casually attended church in their youth, but my sister and I never had to go. I was given the gift of good schooling, but never really committed. My father had his own business, and this was the main driver in my life: to achieve success like his, being able to provide whatever the family needs, and have them want for nothing. I could not have asked for a greater start: I fell into recruitment, and it was the perfect fit of work hard, play hard. I loved it. I was making a huge amount of money, I had all the toys, and was working in a growing business, which took me all over the world. But then it all changed, I moved to Sydney, and faced my life's first major obstacle. It was a significant change of pace of work, and nothing seemed to click. I felt really disconnected from myself, things that used to come easily to me simply did not work anymore. I really hit rock bottom. For the first time, I could not hit my basic work objectives and I crashed.

I found Australia to be a slower lifestyle, and that lifestyle was about living, enjoying the surf and the great outdoors, rather than chasing the endless dreams of more. This is where it changed for me. When I started to suffer, I connected to a much deeper sense of suffering felt in the world all around me. I was watching the news, reading social media, and it all felt like a distraction, a painful misinterpretation of my own life experience. I realised that although technology has been enhancing rapidly in our society, connecting us like never before, we have nevertheless been left feeling empty, struggling and alone. If we were truly living in a civilised society, there would be no homeless people, everyone would have access to the health care they need, and old school, even tribal, community values would be upheld and encouraged for one and all.

We constantly hear about terror from our media, but is this really a fair representation of what is going on in the world around us? There seemed to be a continual message spread, that we are separate from each other, separate by our race, our gender, our colour, our sexual preferences, and, further still, separate from nature. Everywhere I looked I saw a consistent theme: get the money, get the house, get married, get the kids. Sound familiar? This just stopped making sense to me. The world has been suffocating with health and mental problems. We are overwhelmed with choice, living in a society that stretches us to seek more and more. We have the tools and the toys, but our technical capabilities have not been balanced with our spiritual, natural instincts and desires. We have been on the verge of breaking point, so I decided to look beyond this rhetoric: I went on a quest for truth, I wanted to determine what was really going on in the world around us.

This quest has led me on pilgrimages around the world, to work with ancient mystics from different cultures, and to completely change my outlook on the entirety of our universe. In a way, I have been lucky, being single for the majority of my life, I have had the time and opportunity to venture far and wide, as frequently as I have liked. When things have not been going well for me, I have been able to just pack up, leave and travel. But the reality is, I have spent a lot of my life feeling lonely, that I was missing something. I had never connected with a girlfriend that I felt completed me. To be honest, I used to be terribly judgemental. I was quick to find fault in the girls I was dating, something always felt lacking. When you realise that everyone you meet is a reflection of yourself, you start to understand that it is our own insecurities that create rifts between natural flowing relationships.

I had been living by a strict set of codes, a guideline of principles that governed the choices I would make. But clearly, I needed something to change, these rules were just not working anymore. Then came my first trip to Burning Man. I had been told by many "Burners" that this would be a life-changer, and I am slightly embarrassed to sound like a cliche, but here we are: my life was forever changed. I finally let myself go: I opened myself up to alternative possibilities; I said yes to things I'd considered bad, or just generally things that "I" wouldn't do. After all, who was this "I" that I had become? Maybe there was a better way to be me. We all try to control our natures, but just this once, in this place - an adult playground where anything goes - I accepted all that came my way, and experienced what I'd been missing out on. My memories and vision of Burning Man is this: humanity at its best; creative, wild, loving, giving, nurturing, explorative...My structured mind, the voices that usually told me not to do something, protected me from this and that, fell silent; and in this silence, my true self remembered how to play, how to let go. The imagination let soar by new experiences, embracing new possibilities. I was free to express myself, my divine art, and be loved for who I really am. Burning Man ignited the flame of my soul. On my very first day walking around the playa, captivated by the excitement of it all, everywhere I looked I could see creative genius, people playing freely and beautifully embracing one another. Then a random man came over to me, just hugged me, and said, "Welcome Home!". Obviously I didn't realise it at the time, but from that point on, I knew I was home. This is what living life as a human should be. I realised human beings are amazing, so caring, inventive and loving...

So why, with seven billion people, was there so much suffering around?

After I returned from Burning Man, this question burned inside of me. I actually went into a rage. I wanted to understand what was happening in the world around us. I wanted to know who was responsible, and how we could change.

It was easy to find information on corruption and conspiracy theories promoting evil agendas. But I learnt early on that what you seek you generally find, that with the sheer volume of information available to us today, it is easy to argue both sides of any agenda. So I turned my search to hope: to the positive changes that were happening in the world around us; to the extraordinary healing potential of cultures, back to our roots; to the ancient knowledge of our ancestors and the people that were benefiting from that knowledge in our society today.

My passion became to discover the vast nature of human potential, to give humans back to themselves. I had decided to go to war for humanity. To challenge the system that promoted terror, separateness and left so many of us alone and in need of support. Our brothers and sisters of the human race are equal, as much as the animal and plant kingdoms are a part of us, and I was determined to become part of the change that would have us all realise the truth of this, and create a system based on love and justice.

Chapter 2

The Power of Dreams

Although at first look, the world seemed seeped in tragedy, I have actually come to see the beauty in these crises, because I discovered that it is always the darkest hour that precedes the dawn. While I was looking outside of myself, there was just too much noise distracting me from the truth that I was seeking. It was at this time that I discovered the only way to be the change was to make changes from within. Throughout all my research, teachings and discoveries in wellness, insights into our mind and bodies, I started to recognise patterns in the world around me. As I started to challenge myself to higher learning, I began activating extrasensory perceptions. My dreams seemed to have internal meaning to me, about my life, but most importantly, emotional trauma that I had not been paying attention to.

Did you know that your dreams are a way of communicating with your higher self?

I decided it was time to listen to my dreams, to learn from the lessons they share and use them to focus on the most important dream for my future. At the beginning, I found myself swimming in realms of darkness, connecting to my own inner voice and being guided to understand the reasons for it. I was shown memories from my childhood that I had repressed, important moments in time that had set the tone for the man I was to become.

Not only were these dreams becoming a guide to the inner healing that I required, they were also an insight into possible paths and possibilities for my future. They began to show me future events for humanity and also my destiny alongside it. Then it was down to me to choose a journey, and accept the responsibilities and struggles that would come to achieve those goals.

My most idyllic of dreams was born on an Island off the coast of Croatia, under a night sky of more shooting stars than I could count. It was time for me to choose to devote my life to a cause. As an ever-hopeful romantic, the choice turned out to be quite easy: I chose love. So I made a wish that came in two parts, the first part for me, the second for you:

For my part, I wished to be united with my twin flame, the woman I was destined to meet in this lifetime and have a family with her. I wished for that perfect moment when we would meet: at an orchestrated time when both our respective ancestral karma had been overcome individually, creating an energetic union that would eventually lead to an immaculate conception. To honour this divine gift, I pledged that when this wish came true, I would dedicate myself in service to love; that I would teach others to unite with the lovers they were meant to share this life journey with. My spirit guides told me this will be the most difficult challenge I could ever undertake. To that I responded; Game on.

Since then, I have scaled mountains and crossed oceans for love; sought out gurus of all faiths, sharing in their beliefs, enjoying their magical viewpoints; all the while honing in on my divine truth. I have been sent on vision quests, performed sacred missions around the world, activating ancient ceremonial sites. Using my heart's desire, acting as a living expression of love, in order to bring balance and harmony where there was once pain and corruption. Through it all, my dream woman and I have been turning up in each other's dreams, drawn to each other, flame to flame; taking on different forms, disguising each other's nightly voyages, stealing moments of bliss, whilst leaving little clues showing the way home. I am ecstatic to reveal that my wish was granted. But before it was, I had to earn this divine gift. I had to prove myself worthy. Most importantly, I have found a profound sense of who I am:

- I have become a healer of the mind, body and spirit.
- I have connected with the ancestral power of our earth to channel universal energy in deep meditative states.
- I have been acknowledged in the spirit world as a shepherd of spiritual ascension.
- I have mastered ancient techniques for activating and upgrading our DNA coding.
- I am now a teacher, a poet, a dancer. Even a hugging angel at sober raves.

I have learnt to live life in universal flow, not only being blown as a leaf in the wind, but recognising the hidden signs all around: accepting the divine intent and symbolism behind the animals that cross my path; even to know the meaning and stories told by crackling fire. I broke through the illusion of it all. I overcame trickery, energetic entities that tried to distract me, to tempt me away from my one true desire. I opened myself up to universal order and chaos, and strove through the realms of darkness and the light, devoted in my calling, steadfast in my desire to unite with love. It has been a voyage of discovery of galactic proportions, in revealing and ultimately realising my life's purpose: to be a shepherd; to be the light and the way; to help you realise divine truth; and to show you how to find the most important kind of love, love of your own self.

Soon after I had made this wish declaration, and devoted my life to love, I was rewarded with this dream:

I felt myself fly into the sky.
I heard a voice, "Come, Thor."
"Yes, Father", I responded instinctively.
My astral body was directed to a temple, where the aether anointed me 'Shepherd of the People'.

I started to recite sacred ancient rites, swearing in an oath of service. Energy began to pulsate through my body. I knew my hand was held, someone was sitting to the left of me, one in the same, her own words, her own divine pact made. Warm comforting energy engulfed me, but all I saw was darkness. Travelling the higher realms can be like this: it takes time for the senses to adjust. It has taken many a year of devoted service, to raise my consciousness to a place of presence, where you honour and appreciate the grandness of every moment. Within this moment, I knew my destiny was set. I had accepted a responsibility of monumental importance on behalf of humanity. I was pledging myself in service to the people, in service of love. But I would not be doing it alone, at last I was united with my true love, after all the searching, all the prayers, I had finally found her. But uniting with her in a dream is one thing. Manifesting that dream into a reality is quite something else. Yet, I am here to tell you it can be done.

I was set on my quest, to find love, and to defeat the darkness that stood in my way. Being a seeker of truth and a defender of justice became my mantle. It is so funny to write this, but I had let the boyhood wonder overwhelm me and thus I had chosen to live my life as a dream, to live out the fantasy of becoming one of my childhood heroes. I will readily admit that as a boy I had a flair for the mystical: I used to marvel in the realms of mythology, revelling in the adventures of superheroes, but back then, I had no idea of the sheer power of the imagination; that destiny, heroes and villains, the battle of good versus evil, the balance of light and darkness, was all the more real than I could ever have known.

I am going to share with you all of my secrets now. I'm going to show you the door that Morpheus showed to Neo.

I bet you didn't know that 'Morpheus' is the Greek God of dreams! After you've heard what I have to say, you'll understand the power of a dream.

For those of you that dare to dream, I would like to share a passage from the book: "Astonishing the Gods" by Ben Okri. Let this be your guiding light, and promise of wish fulfilment:

"I love your silence. It is so wise. It listens. It invites warmth. I love your loneliness. It is brave. It makes the universe want to protect you. You have a loneliness that all true heroes have, a loneliness that is a deep sea, within which the fishes of mystery dwell. I love your quest. It is noble. It has greatness in it. Only one who is born under a blessed star would set sail across the billowing waves and the wild squalls, because of a dream. I love your dream. It is magical. Only those who truly love and who are truly strong can sustain their lives as a dream. You dwell in your own enchantment. Life throws stones at you, but your love and your dream change those stones into the flowers of discovery. Even if you lose, or are defeated by things, your triumph will always be exemplary. And if no one knows it, then there are places that do. People like you enrich the dreams of the world, and it is dreams that create history. People like you are unknowing transformers of things, protected by your own fairy-tale, by love."

Chapter 3

Spiritual Science and Alchemy

My Mission: Unite with Love and Save the World.

The world around us is always evolving, and it became my mission to learn about nature and humanity's evolution, so that I could adapt and progress to my highest potential. The most important lesson I learned was the only way to make a difference is to change yourself. This is the truth: the answers are all within you.

Look at this fascinating insight from Barbara Hubbard who has written a wonderful book on Conscious Evolution which I highly recommend. From it, we can take five lessons of Evolution:

- Quantum transformations are nature's tradition
- Crises precede transformation
- Holism is inherent in the nature of reality
- Evolution creates beauty, and everything that endures is beautiful
- Evolution raises consciousness and freedom through more complex order

This is what I had to focus on: changing my behaviours to align with raising consciousness. I found this deep urge inside of me to become a superman.

I was on a quest for Arete, an Ancient Greek term (celebrated in Homeric epic, no less) meaning the purposeful pursuit of all-round excellence and, above all, moral virtue. This became my meditation, contemplating all forms of knowledge and how they relate to my own being. How to better myself, my body and my mind. My simple goal: perfection of the spirit and the mastery of life. I was seeking all forms of extraordinary human potential, discovering how to raise my energetic vibrations and consciously attune to universal energy. It is exceptionally important to train both the body and the mind. The more active and healthy you are, the higher you vibrate. Training in martial arts and yoga were fundamental to my own progression, through which I learnt to harness the power of the breath, my chi. I started to experience benefits such as:

Improved wellbeing, reduction in hostility, increased psychic activity, inner calmness, increased respect for life, increased intelligence and memory retention, increased wisdom and an understanding of the circle of life. I was quite literally buzzing with life and energy.

Meditation and yoga had helped me to still my mind, and live more calmly, but then a curious thing happened: as my vitality started to improve, I remembered my love of reading, I had more time and it was a joy to unravel more of the mysteries of the world around me. I became thirsty for knowledge. Out of nowhere, I was reading science books on Chaos theory, learning about Astrophysics and Astrology, how the movements of planets affect energy mechanics, how the setting of the stars and moon when you are born impact your own characteristics and personality traits. I became fascinated by Psychology and Psychotherapy. There is such a problem with mental health in the world around us, it became clear that I had to understand the inner workings of the mind. Carl Jung became my guru in this field. What surprised me most were that his theories were centred around the collective unconscious, acknowledging synchronicity in therapy and unraveling the complexity and implications of the dream state. Then I came across this quote and I knew that I had chosen the right teacher for me.

"Your vision will become clear only when you can look into your own heart. Who looks outside, dreams; who looks inside, awakes." Carl Jung

For those that wish to be the change, and give back to this beautiful world around us, I wholeheartedly advise you to look to your own self-care first. When you have improved your own well being, you will raise your energetic presence to a place of souls' perfection in every moment. This is how you have the largest impact on your target area of intention and desire. This is also how to discover the universal art of alchemy. You will have heard of alchemists before, typically associated with the transmutation of common metals into gold, and seeking the elixir of life, a remedy that would cure all diseases and prolong life indefinitely.

Through meditation and mindfulness practices, I discovered the truth of these ancient mysteries, that in deep states of relaxation and self-reflection, you can tune into sensory reactions to mindful assessment of the body, and relieve stress and pains from areas of tension. I learned that the alchemists' famous furnace, an athanor, can also be interpreted as his stomach. Indian scripture describes the stomach, or solar plexus, as the body's second mind. You can think of it as connecting with an internal supercomputer; that a healthy mind and body is the secret to unlocking and utilising this hidden power.

After we learn how to purify our bodies, you will start to communicate with your higher self. You will learn how to reprogram neural pathways in your brain: to activate your extrasensory abilities, all that lies dormant and hidden within your DNA coding. Once you have learnt this, then there will be no more disease, as you will have learnt how to heal your own body. As such, the search for the elixir of life, otherwise known as the holy grail, is in fact the search for enlightenment. These are not buried treasures at ancient sites, they are not in lost cities of gold (well, at least, not in this physical realm). They are, in fact, a state of being in your own self.

A true alchemist would never need gold. They find their gold within divine contemplation and life experience. It is within their essence of light, union of the mind, body and spirit where they harness their own golden inheritance and power.

Chapter 4

Performing Alchemy within your Dreams

Lucid dreaming occurs in a sleeping state, when your awareness effectively wakes and you realise that you are, in fact, dreaming. From this point on, you can play an interactive role in the dreamscape: taking control of the environments and people around you, even choosing the exact adventures that you wish to journey upon. You can choose any scenario to experience: you can drive the fastest cars in the world, you can fly, you can have sex with any and all of your celebrity crushes. The dream realm is a divine playground where you can experience every sense and delight, but it is so much more than that. It is a place where all thoughts, emotions and events from all time are occurring at once. Some people know it as the akashic records, a library to visit and download information about yourself, and the universe.

We spend approximately a third of our life asleep - that could be up to 30 years worth! Would you not like to use that time more purposefully? Would you like to learn the Japanese language while you are sleeping? Maybe you have always wanted to be able to play the guitar or drums? This is where you can reconnect with your wildest desires, remember your hidden skills, learn how to really express your unique creative talents in all of your living moments.

Before you get to that stage, you'll need to learn how to become a master of being you.

Consider how you see yourself now, and your highest state of being, expressed within an iceberg. You are currently existing as the tip of this iceberg, all that is above the water. What is below the water is the much larger and connected plane of discovery. All the data stored of your memories in this life, how you were held as a baby, the types of foods you were allergic to, even the medicines that your body adapted to and used in your recovery from illnesses. By practising meditation, stilling your mind, you can start communicating with your higher self. In this deep state of reflection, you can start to access these memories. One part of this will involve communicating with your inner child, and coming to terms with internal dramas. You will start to realise that your negative habits and disruptive behaviours all stem from emotional trauma, and ancestral blockages that you have been ignoring all your life. These manifest as distractions affecting your current decisions and life choices, which can lead to an almost constant state of dissatisfaction. Through prayer and meditation, you will learn to communicate with your own body and spirit. Talk to yourself, ask simple questions like: why are you feeling stressed and anxious? Consider it an opportunity to start taking responsibility for the way you think, feel and act. By just telling yourself that you are going to make positive changes, that you are ready to heal the pains from the past, you will have begun one of the most important dialogues of your life. During this process, it is important to set intentions for the future. I would often ask questions that my future self would know and respond to: looking for advice on how I could adapt and change through the healing process. We face many obstacles in life, and I liked the idea that I could ask my guardian angel to help me prepare for those challenging moments.

One of my most memorable and rewarding experiences came during my pilgrimage around India. I was really stuck on some trust issues: I was struggling with a lot of contradictory dream messages, my head was filled with voices, and I could not decide how to move forward, I even questioned whether I should continue on this path at all. I was overwhelmed, but as fate, spirit, or luck would have it, I found myself at a Ganesha temple. The Great Elephant spirit had come to me in a vision before, and I was learning that Ganesha had long been a guiding light for me. He is praised as the remover of obstacles, the patron of arts and sciences and the deva of intellect and wisdom. So I said a simple prayer asking for this confusing obstacle to be removed. Miraculously by the next night it was. Finally a powerful voice within that had been distracting me, daring me to give up, was silenced for ever more.

You will find that you do not always have to understand exactly why you are feeling a certain way, it is all about the way you choose to handle the situation. It is important to take your dreams as a calling for action on how you can change the way you think and act on a moment by moment basis. You begin the initiation of dream therapy by committing to the process. Get a journal to track your experiences, taking note of how you felt during and after waking. Then throughout your daily life start making assumptions about what you are being told and what actions are being advised. Only when you heed those messages; when you quit the addictions that plague those dream scenarios, will you start to heal both inside and out.

Interpreting Dreams

Dream therapy and observation is not a straightforward, linear practice. You may have a dream that lasts twenty minutes, and it is full of action and events, but the last thing you experience, the last spoken word that you heard and remember when you wake may be the only important message that you needed to hear. The goal is to raise conscious awareness when waking up in new dream states. It's difficult at first, I started with only fleeting memories of my dreams. This is where writing a journal comes into its own. I stress the importance of writing even the smallest-related element that you can remember. When lucid dreaming, you will find that you are not quite yourself, that you actually do not have full awareness, and it is exceptionally difficult to remember exactly what is going on. You will have to learn that it is not just the events that you need to record, but also your feelings, the characters that you interact with, and what they might represent to you. Interpreting dreams is challenging, and in the end only you can know the truth.

Let me give you an example: for about nine months, I had a recurring dream. I was in chains, surrounded by aliens, and I was being restricted from getting to my dream woman. I was always fighting with these aliens, raging at them, pleading with them to let us go, or even for us to just spend a moment together. One night I had a really painful interaction with them, I was taken into her cell in chains, I tried to reach out to her and tell her it would be ok. But just as I did, the dream broke and I woke up. It was terribly frustrating, but I focused on the practice, and got up to write it all down. As I did, I opened the page and noticed a drawing I had made about activating the chakra system. I had made a note about forgiveness being the divine response to all action, which got me thinking, so I got myself into a meditative state: from my perspective, I sent a message to these captors, something along the lines of "I don't know who you are or what you are doing, but I forgive you. I am not sure how this works, why we are in this situation, but I forgive you." It was a difficult thing to do, yet at the same time, it came naturally and made sense in that moment. Immediately after this, I had a vision of my father. He smiled at me and gave me the thumbs up. After which I felt a pulse of energy beat in my heart. Intuitively, I just knew that the whole drama of chasing this woman, and fighting captors was, in fact, related to an inner childhood pain that I had been repressing. I had finally forgiven my father for something that was in my unconscious. From here, I started to view my dreams as mostly facing my shadow self, and the darkness being feelings that I had been suppressing. I started learning ancient meditative breathing techniques, adapting these with my own interpretations, teaching myself to self heal. I would get myself into a meditative trance before sleep, focussing on dreams that I didn't understand, or even analysing why I had trust and shame issues; then I would go into the dream experience, and be taught the reasons for those pains, and even advised on how to bring peace to the past.

An important point to make here is that revelations of these dream memories and experiences can occur at any time. For example, you may have a dream that only makes sense a year later. Equally I have been able to analyse the same dream, where my father was putting too much pressure on me, in two different ways. The first time I got the impression that I needed to confront him, so I did. Then six months later, I had the same dream, but I knew that I had to forgive him this time around. As we evolve on our journey, we achieve higher states of understanding, and through this, our action and response to the same thing changes.

Ancient Knowledge

Within our body we have chakra centres which energy flows through. In Sanskrit, 'chakra' can be interpreted as "wheel". There are seven of these points in our bodies, each governed by spiritual laws, levels of consciousness, and blocked by negative emotional attachments. Through dream therapy, I eventually learned how to bring awareness to blocked trauma, leading to balancing my whole chakra system*.

Once you have gone through your own chakra self-healing, the real fun begins. Lying dormant at the base of our chakra system, within our root lies the kundalini. In many cultures, it is known as serpent energy, and it starts to rise and enhance your spiritual awakening once you have begun to practise these forms of healing and meditations.

This serpent imagery is important. Archaeologists around the world have discovered monuments from different civilisations from a range of eras through time, all with symbols of serpents rising on their artefacts and temples.

*Please see appendix A, for a secret guide on unlocking the chakra system

On top of this, I have made a special point of highlighting that the chakra points are represented by the colours of the rainbow.

These are not coincidences.

So time to get daring; let's discuss some out-of-world experiences I have had and link those with ancient prophecies for the future of humanity.

Chapter 5

Awakening our Spiritual Powers

You cannot go far these days without hearing someone talking about 'awakening'. In my terms, this is when an individual starts to get a sense of something much grander going on in the world around them. You start to pick up deeper intuitions calling to you from within, awakening to inner guidance that wants you to question life. We live in a world ruled by the mind, but this deeper call comes from our hearts and is screaming at us to pay attention to our emotions and feelings. For me, at the beginning of this journey, I started to get a real sense that I am not from here, that this is not really my home. I started to notice just how different I was from my family. I guess for the most part, I was becoming disconnected to the person I had been raised to be, the person my family thought I was, how I should act, work, even the very goals I should aspire to.

It was time to open up and listen to the world around me, and when I did, I became very sensitive to pain and suffering. I was learning more about my true self, I was becoming purer, more spiritually attuned. If you find yourself in a similar situation, this is the time to do two things: find the power in solitude embracing all moments by yourself, and to be with people that uplift your spirit. It is also a time to get closer to your family. But there is a problem with this. You will find that a lot of your emotional trauma is from your childhood, which is directly manifested in the presence of your parents and siblings. For instance, in the nine months gestation period of your birth, you are significantly affected by the emotional state of your parents. Their thoughts, fears, pains, and joys are encrypted into your very genes, so if your father is distant or overbearing at this time, the way your mother responds to this, feeling alone, abandoned or suffocated will become an inherited karmic trait that will begin to form part of your personality. This is how deep it goes.

I will go into this a bit more later, but the key to becoming enlightened and finding peace is inner knowing and acceptance. It is not about assigning blame to why you are in this position, it is about taking action: to self-analyse and understand the traits that make you feel a certain way and to act accordingly to overcome the situation you find yourself in. It is your choice, choose to blame your past, your parents, society, or wake up, find the reasons to be grateful, act as your highest self, expressing your divinity through forgiveness and compassion.

Astral Voyaging

Once I had conquered my fears and anxieties from my childhood, I was ready for my first out-of-body experience, commonly known as astral projection. My energetic vibrations were syncing with those of the spiritual world. The door between the realms was open, and I literally flew straight through it. It is quite difficult to explain what astral projection is and all that it means to me. But let's try for fun. Consider that you have two bodies, one your physical, and the other a 'light body', which is a vehicle you can use to journey with. In deep meditative states, and dream experiences, you can transfer your awareness from the physical into this vehicle and voyage through the entire universe. During these trips, you will experience different senses, visions and insights into the cosmos, awakening a host of memories locked within you, encoded in your DNA waiting for you to rediscover them.

This is how I begun, it was the middle of the day and I fell asleep after listening to a guided meditation. I knew I was asleep, but I could also tell that I was in the room and feel my body lying on the bed, my body began to stiffen, and energy was pulsating all over me. It was almost like I was getting heavier, sinking into the bed itself. Then boom, my 'light body' and awareness shot right up through the room and out into the sky above and beyond. This was not a visual experience, I just knew that I was flying in space. Although I could still feel a part of my body, I also realised that it would not be as simple as opening my eyes and waking up. In order to do that I would quite literally have to fly back down into my room. I heard two voices: a woman and a man. Then I saw the face of a grandfather-type figure, who showed me a piece of scripture, I believe written in Sanskrit. He asked if I could translate it, but I could not. So I just said no, and that was that, because in truth all I really wanted to do was fly around in space. Come on, don't tell me that is not what you would do!

From there I was hooked. When I was not working, I was trying to figure out what had just happened, and how to do it again. However, then the real trial by fire began. In the following dreams, I found myself in chains, going to a sort of interrogation centre in the sky. This was concerning. In general, I was increasingly worried about government corruption and corporate greed that was controlling the distribution of wealth and power down here, but up in the aether as well? That surprised me. I even found myself locked up in a jail on my first few astral travels. I didn't know why I was in chains, I didn't know who the jailors were, and I was starting to get scared. But I was determined to find out, so I thought, "you know what, at least if I'm up there and interacting with them, maybe, just maybe I can figure out how to escape, take back control, and fight for freedom". So I reached deeply within, found the courage to return to this realm and face these jailers. I told myself I am prepared for this, recited my power prayers and got into a trance state ready to face them.

This determination and desire for justice must have made quite an impact!

Instead, I woke up in a forgotten but familiar orchard, (I got the feeling that this was from a past life of mine). I walked around and was attracted to a huge tree, as I climbed inside I noticed it was inscribed with the word 'Might'. From there, I went for a stroll, enjoyed the fruits of the forest, literally plucking and tasting the fruit that was around me - it tastes just as real, if not even better than fruit from here – and just as it was time to leave and return to my body, I noticed a table with two individuals sitting at it. I did not think they could hear me, but I overheard them say "he is brave". This was pivotal for me, quite possibly the driving words that have inspired me to spend years travelling around the astral realm from that point on.

There have been lots of experiences like these, I hear different voices, being directed this way and that. The places seem quite natural, but at the same time different. Words can appear from nowhere, strange senses and feelings blend into the experience. One time, I was instructed to head into a Golden Forest, so off I charged. I do not why, but I reached behind my back and found a sword there, and I just laughed while swinging it around ready for what was to come. I ended up in a fortress, facing a strategy maze with stone soldiers that I had to get past. It was in this moment that I realised I had been here before, but this time around I was more prepared for the challenge. My meditation practice had taught me how to calmly react to the scene before me, so I was able to win my way through. For my reward, I came face to face with the most beautiful woman I had ever seen in my life. She looked at me, we fell to the ground together, and I heard the words, "I knew you would come." This was my dream woman, my twin flame, manifested right into my arms. It was only a fleeting moment, but for me, from that point on I know that we were united forever in our palace in the aether; that my wish had been heard, and that the dream challenges were obstacles for us to face as we drew closer and closer to our destiny when we would finally meet in the physical world.

So you see, dreams really can come true.

The dream world has become a place of conscious connectivity for me, the limitless imagination set free to wildly play with all else who dare to venture in these depths. You could consider it something alikening to a virtual game, where you have to pass tests to ascend to higher levels.

Each adventure offers a teaching for you, and you get to decide how to incorporate that lesson into your waking life, which will in turn advance the dream scopes of your future.

I believe the next stage of human evolution is to understand the dream world, this super conscious place of connectivity. This is part of the spiritual ascension process our world is currently transcending into. The great awakening of humanity, as we learn the truth about all the energetic life-forces that exist throughout our universe. As we evolve, heightening all our senses of perception, enhancing our human potential, all the while remembering how to interact and communicate within this dream state, beginning our own journeys of personal discovery, and transforming the very nature of the life that we wish to lead.

Synching with Spirit

Throughout the process of conscious ascension, you will start to activate extrasensory skills and powers. You will begin to experience an increase in psychic activity. You may encounter or already be familiar with mediums, gifted individuals that can communicate with the spirit world. In my terms, this is about becoming consciously aware of your senses, and training yourself to recognise all of the signs, omens and energetic activity that is occurring around you. This is part of the process of channeling with spirit. When you start to notice signs all around you, acknowledging messengers in every shape and sense, revealing the divine intent hidden in serendipitous moments. It was very liberating for me to discover that, in fact, synchronicity is all just part of the plan. I have been acknowledging visions and messages from spirit for a long time now. This has occurred in lots of ways, mostly in the dream state, but I have also been passed messages through books, movies, even music from a car radio speaks to me. But my favourite is to read and interpret the messages flowing in nature, through our wind, water, fire and all her glorious creatures.

I have come to know that I have many spirit guides, some of these appear to me as animals, some as gods from different religions some even as guardian angels. I do not just have to be in a dream state to hear their calls, sometimes I just close my eyes and focus on a particular guide and reach out to them, letting the voices and feelings that arise be the message that I need to hear at that time. I see them as a symbol of guardianship. Some as gatekeepers to higher levels of understanding, and others just as a gentle reminder that I am not alone, that I am always held and protected by a higher power that loves me. It became important for me to learn about my particular guides, ones that were linked to my ancestral lineage. When you start to wander in the higher realms, you will start to interact with lots of different entities and beings, it is key that you get comfortable with who it is that you choose to journey with.

Spirit now reveals to me in all shapes and sizes. For those that are open to this, you start to appreciate the animals crossing your path and the secrets they have to share with you. Spiders have deep connections to the underworld, our grandmother spirit where hidden wisdom resides. Snakes reveal opportunities for transformation, the shift of old thinking to new freedoms. Birds have unique traits, differing birdsongs altogether make up the sweet melody of our soul. I particularly relate to Robins, they are always flying around me, bringing me love notes from my lady. Robins are typically associated with rebirth, and I've been reborn again and again in my quest of ascension, as we drew closer together from each meeting. In most cases, the choice will be yours whether you choose to embrace your gifts, acknowledge a grander sense of yourself, and start to build your own personal and wider view and knowing of universal wonder. However, for some of you it will not be a choice. I believe this is the next stage of human evolution, we have all incarnated here at this time in order to perform certain tasks. Although it may be painful now, and you may sense the truth of what I am saying, the building of a pressure inside. Until you face it, and become one with it, you will be worse from hiding from it. In effect, a medium will be interacting with energy. They may perceive that energy as a person that is recently passed for example, but that energy will come to them in many different forms, they might hear voices in their head, see auras and colours around trees or people, they might see vibrating balls of light. The key is how they interpret these energetic experiences, and relay information and messages to the people ready and waiting to hear them. It is important to let your intuition lead you in this process. Go with your feelings, listen to your heart not your head. Psychics have opened to this phenomenon, knowing that intuition does not reside in the mind. To be psychic, you have got to be out of your mind, because intuition resides in the psyche, the realm of the soul.

Chapter 6

Discovering your Creative Genius

One of the most enjoyable parts of this ascension process, is in the rediscovery of your unique creativity. It is time to embrace your inner wild. We all have a mix of feminine and masculine qualities within us, and it is important to recognise these and be truthful with yourself, own up to which qualities are your strengths and which ones need improvements. Think of it in terms of Ancient Taoism, looking at the concept of Yin and Yang. Life can be viewed as an exchange of energy, for every state of being exists within a complementary state of flow. Yang, masculine energy expresses itself through, initiation, logical analysis, domination, directed force. Yin, its feminine counterpoint responds to this exchange through receiving, intuition, uncontrolled passion and flow. The idea being that you must truly analyse every aspect of yourself, and find the highest state of being in response to all situations that you find yourself in. You need to realise that you have both aspects of yin and yang within you, and sometimes there's a need to take control of your life, and other times to surrender to the unknown.

Once you have stopped viewing yourself in terms of how others perceive you to be, how society has depicted the ideal man or woman to look and act, you are left free to be you. Trust me, you will be surprised and energised by finding this freedom of self-expression. There is a whole beautiful world out there just waiting to share in the wonder of your creations. It has led me to some outrageous and wild quirky events. Burning Man was just the start. After which I became a Hugging Angel at Morning Gloryville, a sober rave revolution in London. At 6am people are up, wearing sparkly leggings, queuing for glitter, with yoga on one side and funky upbeat dancing everywhere else… and it was my job to hug everyone as they enter into the event. Now that, for me, is winning at life. I had started to join dance groups, such as 5Rhythms, loving that these were safe spaces to connect and express yourself freely. The music just plays and you flow with it. No judgement of how crazy you choose to move. No talking; you dance by yourself, and when the timing is right, you will glide into the path of a partner and synch into each other's rhythm. My spirit was lighting up. I was meeting new people, and experiencing a whole new side to myself. Then, out of nowhere, one of these new friends invited me to write a poem at an event she was hosting. It surprised me how naturally and quickly I was able to write one, and I would like to share it now, as it is all about coming to terms with your true self.

The Warrior Poet

We are all warriors.
Life is hard.
That's the proof,
we are still standing.

We're on a battlefield!
We are the enemy!
It's not our fault,
that's just the way it is.

We fear everything!
You're afraid right now
You just don't know it
You've taught yourself not to realise it

You've come so far!
You've fought so hard!
But did you remember?
Did you wake to the truth.

You'll know if you did.
I know; because I'm free
I know because I am not afraid
I faced my demons, and I won!

They told me I wasn't good enough
They told me I couldn't do it
You're different, You're crazy
What will everyone else think?

They had a point;
I'd always done things a certain way
The way I'd been taught
The way things have always been done

But I couldn't stand for that.
I didn't see benevolence;
I didn't see a world filled with,
honour, truth, justice.

I couldn't look myself in the mirror
And say, this is all I can be
This is all I have to offer
As good as it gets.

So I started to dream
To let my imagination flow
To seek my own truth;
A way to live in grace and gentleness

It wasn't long before I discovered,
That I was a prisoner,
My very own thoughts betrayed me
Were keeping me under lock and key

Just keep fighting they were saying
Work hard now,
You'll reap the benefit tomorrow
Push yourself, you'll get there

But where is there?
Why does it have to be so hard
What's wrong with softness?
Who's in charge here?

I was angry, frustrated,
Imprisoned by fear, guilt, shame,
My demons were winning!
Until I dared to face them.

Some of you are fighting still, I can tell.

It's the eyes that give you away

How often can you gaze into another's eyes fully;

Deeply, meaningfully, freely opening up your soul to them.

Forgive me if I'm wrong

I mean no offence, I just want you to know who you are

Know how you can be

How you can live, free…

This is my warriors oath:

To know thyself

To protect the weak from evil strong

To be the change.

The Rainbow Prophecy

Let me share with you an ancient native writing I came across known as the Rainbow Prophecy;

"One day... there would come a time, when the earth being ravaged and polluted, the forests being destroyed, the birds would fall from the air, the waters would be blackened, the fish being poisoned in the streams, and the trees would no longer be, mankind as we would know it would all but cease to exist"

Which leads onto:

"There will come a day when people of all races, colours, and creeds will put aside their differences. They will come together in love, joining hands in unification, to heal the Earth and all Her children. They will move over the Earth like a great Whirling Rainbow, bringing peace, understanding and healing everywhere they go."

I am a Rainbow Warrior.

These people have risen.

I hope you hear this as your calling to join our tribe.

Chapter 7

This is the Challenge of Challenges

The journey of ascension and enlightenment is no easy task. Far from it, it can be the most mind shattering, confusing, thought-provoking and even stressful processes to go through, but this book has not just come to you; that is not how this works. It was time for you to hear what is written, for you to know your true self. I promise you, that you are more powerful than you can possibly imagine. It is time for you to uncover the mysteries of your soul, to know your special gifts, the power hidden within you. You most likely sense this, but have not quite figured out what it is, and if you have, not how best to use and enhance them. After you have faced your fears and anxieties, looked at the world through your own eyes without any prejudice, purely viewing the world as you alone can see it, then you will know enlightenment. You will know freedom.

This is a complex game: your spirit guides, your higher self, are all communicating with you from a place of all-knowing. They are in the future, they are in your past. They know what you can endure, how vital it is that you remember all your strength, that you struggle through the illusions, that you find the most precious of treasures buried deep inside. The messages can be unclear, and come through in all shapes and senses. The moments of joy and levity are drowned within the transition that comes from the ascension process. I have been given information that has led me to believe beyond a shadow of a doubt that if I do certain things, go to the places I am told to, I shall finally meet my lady or find all-knowing teachers that reveal answers and send me on to the next stage. I have heard her calling to me, telling me it will be over soon, promised it is the last time, one last sacred mission and all will be well. I was told to fly to Salem, Massachusetts, I was shocked, I only had about £100 in my bank, and this was the third or fourth time the voices had said it was the last time. But I knew of the Salem witch trials, I knew there had been suffering there, and I knew that I had the power to bring love and light to those energetic portals. So I dug deep, I asked friends and family for financial assistance, which they fortunately gave me, and I set off. The experience was sensational! But she was not there, I did not find a teacher, and it was not the last time…

Although frustrating and disappointing, it is part of the process, and there are valuable lessons hidden within those additional layers of confusion and pain. Most importantly, to be careful about managing expectations. I was focussing too much on what I was going to get out of the situation, rather than delighting in the mystery of the adventure itself. I guess I was expecting a type of reward for putting in the effort, doing the deeds I was tasked with. It took me a while to realise that is not how this works. Looking back, this was why I found it so confusing, and also why I was struggling with trusting the guidance itself. Ultimately, spirit was not purposely misdirecting me. That is just how I've experienced it. Truthfully, it has all but destroyed me on so many occasions. This journey has shaken my very perception of reality, the knowledge of everything I ever knew. Anything I thought was a solid foundation to expect, that this is this and that that, I've been shown its opposite, and had my mind opened and blown in so many ways. My interpretation is this, humans are struggling at this moment in time, because we focus too much on the calculability of the mind. We choose order and structure because it is quantifiable. Well, that is not the case for the spirit world. From my experience, we do not yet fully process all the activation and sensory perceptibility to know outright a structured and quantifiable scientific basis for interpretation of the souls realm. Therefore the path of awakening, illumination and enlightenment is challenging because you have to let go of knowing anything. This is how I experienced not knowing, and it was devastating. I experienced it as misdirection, a setting for false hope, and a crushing reality of non-manifestation. I literally read all the books, followed the visions and messages that came through, honoured the guidance. I sacrificed, I pledged myself for the greater good. Accepted the back and forth, even though in the physical sense it felt unending, leaving me in desperate hope of revelation. It has left me internally questioning my sanity. I have upset and lost friends from the process, leaving me feeling confused and more alone. Fortunately my true friends and family are lovingly supportive, but certainly sacred for me. This is a journey for you, and you alone.

It has pushed me beyond the point of comprehension of anything. I have come face to face with demons, aliens, all different sorts of spirit. All the while never receiving explanation of who I was interacting with, which paths I was walking, and when it would end. I am just trying to do good I would say over and over. But most of the time you won't be able to perceive the actuality of your actions, the multi-dimensional ripple effect that you are having on the universe. The ultimate good that you are causing, despite the suffering that you will be subject to. The Buddha says that life is suffering; but that this suffering can be overcome. I have suffered in this quest. I am stronger for it, but I have suffered more than I will ever let on.

When in pain these have been words of comfort to me from Muhammad Ali:

> "S/He who is not courageous enough to take risks will accomplish nothing in life."

I am at a point of knowing. By which I mean I know the depths of who I am as Neil Greenwood. I feel that I have been tried and tested by the universe, and it is at this point I have made a stand. I know what I stand for, I know how much strength, courage, perseverance and devotion it has taken me to get here. All of which I can call upon again, when needed, but I am also willing to concede that at any moment, the next test or trial I face, may lead me to reevaluate what I think I know all over again. You will experience this process in a completely unique way for yourself, which no one else will ever be able to fully comprehend. You will come across people on similar paths as you, you will share stories, and each token of advice will complement your understanding of what you are going through. So in that sense, you will always have support, as we are all each other's teachers and students. Just make sure to enjoy your uniqueness. Take pleasure and pride in your own peculiar way of looking at life, while contemplating these divine and extraordinary experiences.

Honour spirit and you'll be comforted with their guidance

Guidance and support is all around you, as the creator you get to decide how you interact with the spirit world. The amount that you open up to this divine phenomena will be proportional to the experiences that you receive. You may relate to particular heroines from mythology, certain animals in the wild, even your favourite superhero characters will give an indication to your own unique style and gifts. Take time to hone in on a sense of the animals you admire and like to watch in nature. Start to learn about their characteristics, and see how they relate to you, and your current walk of life. It could well be a tiger, which is a symbol of leadership, and likely encouraging you to take charge in your life experience. It could be a whale, which typically spends a lot of time alone in the wild. An indication that your great spirit power is found in stillness and solitude. I have dreams about all kinds of characters, and they all tell a different story, and pass a different lesson. It was only after I had been called 'Thor' and taken to the temple that I started researching Norse mythology. At the time, I had been going through some really painful and confusing dream journeys. I found pleasure and immense strength in a tale I read where Thor was tricked into a set of challenges against one of his foes, the Giant King, Utgard-oki. The challenges turned out to be illusions, and so he was set to fail from the beginning. Thor had a reputation for being hot-headed, and always ready to throw his hammer first and think about consequence later. In the end, Thor, learnt a valuable lesson, to distinguish his actions based on humility rather than hubris. Instead of losing himself to rage at his failing, he learnt that not everything was in his control. That greater forces are at work in this world, and all one can really control is the response to the situations you find yourself in.

I can relate to this immensely, consider me, flying around the aether on this crusade for justice, but I was not looking at the larger picture. I was oblivious to the fact that some cruel actions can actually be acts of kindness which lead to the greater good in the long run. I kept shouting at my guides telling them that this was not fair, I was demanding revelation, explanations for what was going on, but the greater good turned out to be lessons of patience and trust.

That is how this game is played.

Chapter 8

Let's delve into the Mystical for a moment

What follows is an account of one of the realms I've visited:

It is possibly one of the most stimulating experiences that I have ever had, and one that has pretty much set precedent on my beliefs and dreams for the future.

It is clear that whatever the mind perceives becomes a sense of reality. So please bear in mind that all I have written is based on my own sensory experiences. You can choose to believe them, or not. This is my truth. You decide what is true for yourself. I have come to a place of knowing, where all I know is that I really cannot be certain of anything any more.

I shall call in a little support from Socrates here:

"The only true wisdom is in knowing you know nothing"

One night in a dream, I found myself searching through what I can only describe as an Alice in Wonderland rabbit hole, opening and passing through doorways, until I found myself face to face with a dragon. It was massive, it was grey. In truth, I found it more beautiful than terrifying. But for some reason I felt compelled to charge at it. I cannot even explain why, but I guess at that time my instinctive nature was still looking for a fight, and so I just went into attack mode. Fortunately, I heard a very distinctive voice inside my head say "No don't, that wizard is too powerful." It was the first time I had heard a voice in my head, and considering I was running head long at a dragon, it sounded like quite reasonable advice, so I heeded it, and decided to run in the opposite direction instead. I found cover, and noticed a huge beak move towards me, as it opened to potentially bite me. I closed its mouth, and noticed it was a gigantic bird, and patted it reassuringly so that it calmed down. A little weird right, well...What happens next still confuses me, but I looked across the field, noticed a bar, and the barman was holding out a telephone to me, and somehow I knew that was my way out. I rushed over took the call, and as I turned around I noticed a huge amount of movement, there were people and mythical creatures all around me. I can only describe it as an after-party to celebrate the end of an evening's battle. Everyone was laughing and drinking, and in the middle there was a dance floor where I could make out humans and magical beings dancing around. Here is where it gets even crazier: before my awareness started to leave that realm, I had been talking with a satyr. The main words that have always stayed with me, were his adamance that that particular realm was, in fact, the real world.

Do we live in a multi-universe where there is a realm of wizards and mythical creatures?

I embrace my inner weird, so here's a hypothetical wild theory

This is how the journey of a spirit scientist works. Create theorem, have experience, get results, have setbacks, refine the nature of the hypothesis, continue to voyage and discover. Set your wild dreams, flow with them. Dream big, win big. We are living in a significant time of human evolution. The energetic vibrations of the world are rising, and in this process we are collectively connecting with unity consciousness. We are recognising that there is no separation, and learning to appreciate that the kingdom of heaven resides within us. Remember the rainbow prophecy from earlier? Well, a long way into my quest, I came across an additional part of that writing that I hadn't originally noticed:

"Many creatures thought to be extinct or mythical will resurface at this time; the great trees that perished will return almost overnight. All living things will flourish, drawing sustenance from the breast of our Mother, the Earth."

Well my theory is this: the woman I have been chasing, the woman of my dreams, who in turn has chosen me. She is from this mythical realm. I believe that our union has created an energetic explosion of consciousness that is shifting our two realms into one new earth. Science has predicted the possibility of multiple, even infinite realities. Maybe these different realities are, in fact, just different perceptions and levels of consciousness.

My even wilder theory is this, they exist on this new earth now, which is the same earth we exist in, just perceived from a different level of awareness. Whoever is awake and has chosen the path of spirituality, has chosen to go on this journey, and will be able to join this wave of ascension, and live like me and my lady in our realms of possibility and magical potential. Here's hoping anyway. I've been laughing while writing the whole of this chapter. I have come to realise the drastic need for humanity to take life less seriously. We are spiritual beings, here for a life experience. We are here to live joyfully with purpose, co-creating with our fellow beings. Check out every single guru from any tradition in the world, and they will say the same. Seek peace, seek joy, seek happiness, and fulfilment; that you are God, the Creator, whatever you choose to experience is your reality to enjoy.

I have fantastical beliefs and theories, but these are based on my actual life experiences, both in this physical realm and through my years of dream journeying. It is fun for me to believe in this. It is a joy for me to play the game differently to everyone else, but know this: more and more people are seeing rainbows and unicorns in the world around us. I am a dreamer, I am wild. I have done this for me, I have done this for you. I hope that this book has sparked some interest. I do not mind if you think I am crazy. I just hope that you have the strength and courage to follow your own dreams.

The Future as I see it; a Rainbow society

Navajo-Hopi Prophecy of the Whirling Rainbow

"The great spiritual Teachers who walked the Earth and taught the basics of the truths of the Whirling Rainbow Prophecy will return and walk amongst us once more, sharing their power and understanding with all. We will learn how to see and hear in a sacred manner. Men and women will be equals in the way Creator intended them to be; all children will be safe anywhere they want to go. Elders will be respected and valued for their contributions to life. Their wisdom will be sought out. The whole Human race will be called The People and there will be no more war, sickness or hunger forever."

I have connected deeply with the teachings from Neal Donald Washes' writing on Conversations with God, which I highly recommend. I found that his narrative with God really connected with my own highest understanding of what God meant to me. Also, more importantly, it became a fundamental guiding light on interpreting the life of a human in relation to a grander vision of the cosmic self and our future. I heard the word of God when reading his books, and loved the lessons portrayed on how to live a life of abundance in line with glorious creation. Incorporating schools of thought explained, with ancient prophecies and my dreams, I imagine our future society to be a rainbow civilisation. In this future economy, you will not do things for personal profit, but for personal growth, which will be your profit. Profit in material terms will come to you as you become a bigger and grander version of who you really are. Our world will be divided into national states, clusters that interact in a co-creative manner. There will be no government, no laws, just mutual agreements shared between councils of elders based on a code of: Awareness, Honesty, and Responsibility.

Elders will look after the teachings for the community as they have the most experience. The youngster generations will be off discovering their creative talents, and the maturing adults will be energetically engaged with past times and joyful labours that they have chosen for themselves. Chosen shepherds, medicine men and women of the communities will be responsible for communicating with the higher realms guiding through further stages of ascension and evolution. But everyone will be directly interacting with nature, communicating with spirit to their own level of skill and desire. You will be able to reach out and connect with soul mates, unite with your twin flames, learn and experience love and ecstasy in a truly divine sense. We will have become masters of ourselves, knowing when it is time to join a committed relationship, one where your own individuality is cherished, and the goal of each is to help nurture and develop both their own self, and their partners. We will know when our bodies are fertile, and we will be able to dictate the time and place to bring children into the world. At this point, we will have learnt how to communicate with other beings that are looking to have a human experience. In this sense, you will both choose the parental and child groups that you want to incarnate into.

Who are these other beings? Time to contemplate my wild beliefs again.

Chapter 9

We are not alone in this Galaxy

I know it is only a matter of time before we all recognise our cosmic brothers and sisters of this universe. That indeed there is life, vast intelligence throughout our cosmos. However, I do not believe us to be one of the most technically-advanced races out there. In all honesty, it has been explained to me that we are more like children in the grand scale of it all, which makes sense: we have only just realised that we all need to work together as one species to save and live on the planet that sustains our very lives. I know there to be cosmic forces outside of our world both supporting us and working against our own evolution. It is possible that one of the reasons we have not 'officially' made contact is because the human race has been going through a testing period.

Through my astral voyaging, I have found myself on spaceships interacting with different beings. All that seems to be guiding me to greater understandings. They are really informal, I wouldn't say either cheerful or scary experiences. I usually end up having to pass tests of aptitude and endurance, then get rewarded either by being given information, or by having electric activation pulses surge through my body. The best example I can give is from around the time I changed to a vegan diet. In my dream, I saw tables of vegetarian food, then noticed I was ascending in a lift to another level, upon which I found myself in a doctor's chair and I saw someone operating on my stomach. Shortly after, I was walking around another room, and the number on the door was B12. For those of you that don't know, vegans are typically vitamin B12 deficient, as it is difficult to consume this mineral from a plant-based diet. Therefore I interpreted this dream, as my higher self or spirit guides praising me for the switch to a plant-based diet, hence the ascending in consciousness depicted by the rising lift, but also advising that my body was becoming deficient in B12, passing me the information that I needed to take it as supplements. Ultimately I could either interpret this as I'm literally flying into outer space and being abducted by aliens; or my highest state, my united body, mind and spirit have learnt how to communicate together.

I will make a point here, no one has ever come to me and explained the actual details of all this. I have spent time with great teachers from different religions, spiritual faiths and scientific backgrounds, who all have their own way of perceiving the bigger picture. I was a normal guy, working hard, dreaming of supporting my family and just engaging with life and all its opportunities, but along the way, I really started to pay attention to what was going on around me, and then more importantly what was going on within me. Everything I have learnt, I have either read in a book, fanatically researched online, or just exposed myself to by teaching myself new ways to challenge my mind and body. I searched far and wide, going to seminars or quirky events and speaking to people that have opinions on stuff that I care about. From there I made my own presumptions, backed them up with further research, which led to these spiritual and galactic level experiences, where further information has been shared with me. I heard my calling, and I rose to the challenge. I know that I have been chosen for service of a significant nature on behalf of humanity. This calling came on my recent pilgrimage around India and Nepal. That is when I really noticed a progressive shift in the experiences. It was during this trip that I was transported to the temple in the aether and anointed as a shepherd. At the time, I was travelling around India, I was jumping into and out of up to twelve different dream scenarios a night. Flying around different worlds, exploring different realities, learning about life forces and sentient beings. Eventually finding myself at a huge intergalactic legal court hearing, where I got the impression the ownership and management of our galaxy was being "re-evaluated". There were many interested parties brokering for control of certain aspects of the universe. To my surprise, I was in consideration for a position on this council. There was a group of people behind me advising me on the traditions of the court, teaching me the customs and offerings I had to perform. When the hearing was over we went into a private room, and they told me that they were not human. I asked them who they were, to which they only responded: "Does it matter?" Although mystifying, it didn't, so I just said no.

One night after, I woke to find myself at a sacred meeting, I was carrying a letter with me written in sun language. I passed this to a powerful woman, whom I took to be the leader of this galactic council. The letter made her smile, and somehow I knew it meant that Earth had reached its golden moment in history; that enough people had woken up, and the transcendence into our new world had begun. It was during experiences such as these, where the extraordinary potential within our cellular make up was explained to me; that within our DNA coding we have astral tags, which to begin with lie dormant, in wait for our awakening. Either your codes are set to go off at pre-arranged times during your life experience, or you can choose to start activating these codes and taking responsibility for your own ascension process.

Going back to my earlier description of our 'light body, I came to learn that we all have an aura around us, which is our energy field. Also known as a merkaba, which is described as the divine light vehicle used by masters to tune into the higher realms. "Mer" means Light. "Ka" means Spirit. "Ba" means Body. This again is activated by raising your energetic vibrations to the point where you are purifying the body and upgrading your genetic potential. Thus unraveling your inner powers and leading you to your own unique discovery of universal secrets.

I have worked exceptionally hard to discover these treasures. I have devoted myself, and sacrificed myself for the greater good of all. But I am certainly not alone, I have met many rainbow warriors who have done the same. We can be called lightworkers, healers, psychics, witches, the list goes on. People that dare to be unique and express themselves wildly, I LOVE YOU. It is because of all of you that humanity has shown the rest of the galaxy that we are a race worth saving, that it's now time for us to regain our place in the galactic order.

There are Dangers of Astral Projection

Bouncing around these worlds, is it real? What is going on…

This may all sound like a lot to you. I am talking about magical lands, alien worlds, galactic responsibilities. I am sharing both proven scientific and mystical techniques for meditation and psychiatric therapy, and mixing it all in with a fantastical love story.

Here is why…I want you to know all I have seen, my truth. I also want to fill you with hope, but more than that, I have opened the door for you. You can choose to walk through it or not. If you do I am here for you. All of my tribe are here for you, and we are many. Maybe you're not ready for what comes next. That is totally cool. Not everyone is, but if you are ready to peep through, you are going to need a shepherd, and you are going to need protection.

So if you are still here, let's dive straight into the protection you will need:

This journey is all about finding your own divine truth. Taking the time to care for yourself, and becoming the greatest vision of all you are and can be. Use the tools from this book to empower yourself in all of your moments. Become a fierce tiger if that calls to you, live life and fly around like 'wonder woman' if that inspires and empowers you. When you open up to these possibilities you are going to see beyond what most people can currently comprehend. There are other entities out there, and some of them do not want you to know how powerful you are. By interacting with spirit you are acknowledging these beings, and it is vital when you are offered gifts and knowledge, that you make choices that serve your highest good. Without knowing it, you have likely already accepted energetic contracts that are keeping you in a state of fear, guilt, shame, grief and denial.

A good place to start in a meditation will be to state this important phrase:

"I sever all energetic contracts that restrict my freewill and do not serve my highest purpose."

Let me explain:

After I had flown to this wizard world, the conception of time and space just dissolved for me. I was interacting with different entities, experiencing different timelines, knowing that the decisions I was making would affect the reality of my waking life. I was presented with lots of gifts, all the while being challenged to see what I really wanted. I was offered huge sums of money, extravagant houses, successful businesses, but this didn't seem right to me, so I refused. I took the time to evaluate what would be most important to me, what was the spiritual nourishment that I was looking for. I knew that I would be fulfilled by uniting with this woman, by starting a family with her, and that certainly had nothing to to with riches. So when having these experiences I questioned, is this choice something I truly desire, will this enrich my life with love and purpose, or does the offer come from a place of fear. Am I just being offered choices to indulge me, because I'm not satisfied with all that I am. In my mind I was building the mantle of superman, I was on a crusade for love and justice. I saw myself as choosing light over darkness, choosing to protect the weak from evil strong, which actually led to many dreams about superman, both being him and learning from him.

It even got to the stage where I would get into a dream state and see the superman badge illuminated in the sky. When that would happen I would have to get up, get into a powerful meditation, arm myself with my spiritual gifts, calling on my spiritual guides for strength and protection. Once ready, I would go back into the dream world, and typically find myself in a dark realm. I would then have to shine my light to protect people, or pass people my gifts of knowledge, to help them with their own awakening. This was my reckoning; the energy of the universe is love, so I shall call in power in its purest essence. At first, I questioned why I kept flying into these realms of pain and suffering, but then I realised...my light shines brightest in the dark. It appeared that every interaction in these realms purified my presence and that of my energetic reach to all those beings I encountered. In these dark (lower realms), your light and energetic vibration is extremely attractive to the entities that roam there, so they tend to seek you out and latch onto you. This typically led me to feel like I was in a fight. I was always grabbed from behind, and found myself in a struggle and not being able to wake into my body. Some of you reading this will recognise these symptoms. These experiences are actually very normal, it's commonly termed as sleep paralysis. The dream state is a place of universal connectivity, you are in the game whether you know it or not, and even whether you like it or not. It is my role, to be the shining light that leads the way, and guides you through this process. It is going to be your choice what adventure you wish to go on from here. It is a process of mutual exchange, you will interact with both allies and foes, all the while deciding who you are, and who you want to be. Effectively you will be giving your power to the ones that you engage with the most. So choose wisely.

This is a personal journey for you to discover your own intimacy with spirit, your own life's purpose. Once found, you may actually decide that it is not quite for you, and that is fine too. Because either way, at this point you have found the inner strength within, found a state of self that recognises you are the creator of this reality. That wherever you choose to wander, you are finally back where you were meant to be all along, in the driving seat, master and commander of your own life experience.

Here's a question for you, what is Good and what is Evil?

As I have outlined previously, I have come to know and love my own darkness and harnessed its strength and power. The emotional blockages of the past, my pains, frustrations and anguish that had been raging inside, these were my demons, but by bringing awareness to them, acknowledging my djinn and accepting it as my brother, we became one. I am the darkness that is the light. Because I am what I am, and from there, what I choose to become. We can all recognise control mechanisms around us. The media constantly portrays images of terror and disharmony. These are just tools to manipulate, to distract and repress us into these states of fear and anxiety. But it is our choice whether to consume these narratives or not. I choose to believe the controlling elite have had their day, that their regime of misdirection and darkness is over. I shall tell you outright: there is a much bigger battle of light and darkness going on all around you than you can possibly imagine. Don't just take my word for it though, do your own research, start figuring out what is really going on within you and all around you. Find your own truth, and then make the decision about what to do about it. Because you are involved, and you are likely being manipulated right now.

The choice is, let that continue to be the case? Or choose freedom.

When you go to sleep your awareness (consider it the light ethereal body) travels the souls realm, whether you remember it or not. You are a light being, but the realm of the soul, the superconscious, is a state of totality, a state of harmony, which requires balance. There must be both light and dark, positive and negative, good and evil. You are pure divine light, an energetic lightning rod, which is extremely attractive to dark energy. In effect, you give off a positive vibration, which a negative entity feeds on; that energy knows only to feed. Have you ever heard of energy vampires? Look it up and think along these lines. But you shouldn't be afraid of this revelation, you should be empowered, because now I have explained the game and the rules. By literally sleeping and ignoring these facts, you are letting them just do what comes naturally to them, but by waking up, choosing freedom from this, you will start remembering how to take your power back.

For those of you that are already flying around in the aether having sex with your favourite celebrities, you should definitely think about who that actually is. Your kundalini sex energy is one of the most powerful tools you have in your spiritual war chest. Do not give it away freely. All you need to do is remember that we are the real power. Know this; the only thing in this world to fear, is fear itself. Because the aether, the universe, all energy is love. When you realise this, you'll know God, you'll be the Creator, you'll be free. I am now free to adventure and play in life. I have the largest smile on my face as I tell you that I choose to accept God, Odin, as my father. I have enjoyed wielding the mighty hammer of Thor in my dreams, and all the wild experiences I have had as I have battled my trickster brother Loki around the universe, to prove myself worthy of ascending the throne in that kingdom. Let this be my message to you as Thor; we have lived through Ragnarok. Call it the end of the world. Call it Armageddon. Call it our day of judgement. The truth is right here for you, if you dare to seek it.

The Golden age is here. We are the Rainbow People, our time is now.

Chapter 10

My Conclusions from this awakening

On this path you'll discover your own way of interacting with the world, and go on a journey beyond time and space to the realm of the soul. In general, we start our life lived by the rules and circumstances that we are born into. Those of our family, our upbringing and the society that we live in. We develop awareness, build character and create a perception of ourselves, an understanding of our inner strengths and weaknesses, and what is expected of us.

The awakening is a process of self-reflection. New possibilities and opportunities are presented to us and we start to question what is really going on around. These indulge the darker aspects of our psyche, where we begin to explore the hidden depths of our subconscious. We challenge former perceptions and face repressed emotions within, accepting and overcoming the ancestral karmic blockages passed down from our parents. This is a learning phase, where you begin to remember how to communicate with spirit, facing your fears on your quest for inner peace. This part requires strength. This is where you realise that the darkness, your inner demons, are, in fact, your most powerful allies. They are literally the manifestation of childhood trauma, your inner child that is acting out because you have forgotten to take care of yourself. As you do, you will learn to trust your instincts, those gut feelings and itches that will open up enchanting possibilities. Somewhere during this part you will become overwhelmed with the beauty of all that is, all the wondrous variety of life that surrounds us. You shall remember the interconnectivity of it all, that we are one with nature. You will remember that it is our sworn duty to protect all of earth's creatures great and small. Even the trees, plants and the flowers that breathe life into us everyday, you shall remember that we must live together in harmony. That we are here to create heaven on earth.

At this point, it is time to surrender to universal power and flow. You shall start to hear whispers in your dreams. You will start to recognise signs and messages in the world around. The higher realms are calling to you. Spirit that has been with us all the while is demanding an audience. The time has come for us to put right the wrongs that have been committed throughout the ages. This next part involves ascending your conscious awareness through the superconscious. You will become aware that there is no such thing as time and space, that we are the only ones who perceive time in a linear fashion. This is as much beautiful and fascinating as it is confusing and painful. In this moment, should you choose to continue on this path, you will have to face a new reality, a new conception of yourself. You shall start to shift away from old ways, and patterns of life, even friends and family. Through all of this, you will be reconnecting with divine intent, remembering your sacred vow of service to life and love. You will have remembered your purpose in life. You shall be guided to gifts of power, independent of others, these will be your unique and remarkable talents. Your own creative genius that you were born to express within every waking moment of opportunity.

When you learn to live life expressing your own inner nature and beauty, you will find yourself experiencing joy like never before. You shall be fulfilled, you will know your destiny. There will still be obstacles before you, but you will have gained the strength, guidance and power to overcome all that blocks the way. Enlightenment is a process of becoming, whilst also being. There will still be struggle and pain, but worry no more.

The Result: I'm a Shepherd

It is my belief that we all instinctively, desire peace, prosperity, joy, and fulfilment, that we seek satisfaction and self-expression in all of our labours. In order to achieve this we require health in our bodies and stillness in our minds. To love, and to be loved.

For life to be fulfilling one has to find purpose. This is what I see as the meaning of life. To become one with universal harmony, joyfully existing connected to your natural environment and in awe and admiration of all that is above and beyond our comprehension.

My purpose is to be a shepherd of human and conscious evolution. To be the light and the way to self-actualisation. To share the knowledge, experiences, tools and revelations that have led me to an enlightened state of being. It is my joy and honour to be a guide for humanity through its current phase of spiritual ascension.

These are my Spiritual Observations as a Shepherd

Universal Flow and Power

The source of all creation is pure consciousness. Creative genius is the joyful rhythm of this universal beat. A shepherd's role is to lead you to this flow, so that when you discover your purpose, you align with this power. Then you can manifest your own desires and dreams.

Purpose

Everyone has purpose, these are your unique gifts and special talents. When you blend these with service to others, you experience divine ecstasy and live out the wildest fantasies of our spirit. The privilege of a lifetime is to become who you truly are.

Detachment

Through surrender to the unknown, we discover the wisdom of uncertainty. We free ourselves from the systemic thoughts and emotions that restrict our potential. When we let go of ego attachment, we reconnect to universal flow that orchestrates the dance of the universe.

Karma

Your intentions and desires become ripples for how you think, feel and act. Every action generating a force of energy that returns to you in kind. What we sow is what we reap.

Golden Rule

Do unto others as you would have done to yourself. The universe operates through dynamic exchange. By willingly giving to others what we seek for ourselves, we align with universal abundance and enrich the soul.

Our Kingdom of Heaven

We are born of creation. It is our role to find joy and express our own inner nature, our own genius. In this manner, all of life can be a meditation, in which you are contemplating the divine. Rediscovering our unique contribution to the dance. This is called true wakefulness, or mindfulness.

I have gone through a huge transformation on this journey. I have come to know myself and to love every part of me. All the mistakes and regrets that I thought I had, I have accepted as wonderful lessons to have grown from. My weird peculiarities, my wild and wacky ways that I used to hide from and was ashamed of are, in fact, my strongest attributes, because it is me, all me.

My wish came true. I have remembered to live as an expression of love in all of my moments. To love all those around me as I love myself. This was my dream. That I would know love, and that humanity would live in times of peace and prosperity. This is how I see the world, this is my divine truth.

There are many realms, many kingdoms, all types of sensory experiences available to the willing. For those that wish to share the vision of a united world, a harmonious coexistence, I welcome you to join my dream world.

Come and join me and my lady, the love of my life. Together we are playing in our astral palace offering guidance and healing to those that dare to venture above and beyond. For all those ready to take an active role in humanity's next evolutionary leap.

Find the kingdom of heaven within you. Embrace love in all forms around you, this is your highest state of being when you are dancing with God. Knowing that you are both the creator and the creation.

To win this game, choose your highest state of expression in all of your moments of being. Choose joy in your labours. Choose forgiveness over retaliation. Seek inner wisdom and peace. Dance your heart's desires, live your wildest dreams, play this divine game from a place of empowered knowing.

There's more to share, but for now here's a prayer for us all

Our Mother and Father, Who art amongst us,

Hallowed is Thy presence.

Our realm is here, We sense Thee near,

On Earth, Which is our living Heaven.

Teach us this day to bake our bread,

And accept us in our humanness.

As we accept each other, In spite of our limitations.

Lead us not into domination, But empower us to freedom.

For ours is This Air, This Fire, This Water, This Earth,

Forever and Ever.

We are one, United in nature.

One for all, and all for love.

The Gift of Life

In closing, I'll share my last thoughts. Life itself is the blessing.

Wherever we are, whatever we think we should have achieved, this is all we can be right now in this moment. I intend to treat all of it as a gift.

Experiencing the pain and the suffering along with the joy and the peace. Appreciating the love and the light, just as much as the wildness and the deepest darkest mysterious depths.

I choose to be kind and compassionate to my own self in all of my moments, so that I may be stronger and more freely able to share my love and light with all that I encounter.

I hope that this book has sparked some interest in you. For all those that it has, welcome to the Rainbow tribe.

I would absolutely love to hear from you. Let's share and learn together. I am involved in charitable projects aimed to bring awareness and offer solutions to our society's problems with mental health.

I've included a list of conscious events and retreats that are currently available.

Volunteering Program in Nepal

During my pilgrimage, I worked as a school teacher in a village in Nepal. With our support this village is growing. We have built a new school, and are looking for people to volunteer as teachers.

In the future, there will be opportunities to run an adventure centre there. We are creating rock climbing and abseiling facilities; organising mountain and forest trekking; setting up yoga and meditation retreats.

Check out this link for ways to contribute:
www.gofundme.com/nepalese-school-project

Yoga, Meditation and Mindfulness Events Worldwide

There are many wellbeing festivals, sober raves, all sorts of uplifting and inspiring ways to spend your time laughing and loving. I run a community on facebook that promotes these types of conscious businesses and events.

https://www.facebook.com/echochamberdreams/

Healing and Teacher Profile

Neil Greenwood is a Mindfulness & Meditation Teacher and Spiritual Healer.

Neil is available for private consultations, as well as a keynote speaker for events related to conscious evolution and spiritual ascension.

I welcome you to follow and add me through either of these channels.

LinkedIn:
www.linkedin.com/in/neilgreenwood/

Instagram:
www.instagram.com/neilwgw/

Facebook:
https://www.facebook.com/echochamberdreams/

Reference to books that have helped me on my path

Spiritual

Conversations with God : Neal Donald Walsch
The Power of Now : Eckhart Tolle
Celestine Prophecy : James Redfield

Scientific

Memories, Dreams, Reflections : C. G. Jung
Conscious Evolution : Barbara Marx Hubbard
A New Vision of Astrology : A.T. Mann
Tao of Chaos : Katya Walter
Death by Black Hole : Neil DeGrasse Tyson
The Last Hours of Ancient Sunlight : Thom Hartmann

Magical / Mythical

Astonishing the Gods : Ben Okri
The Alchemist : Paulo Coelho
The Night Circus : Erin Morgenstern

Inspirational

The Power of One : Bryce Courtenay
The Last Lecture : Randy Pausch
Zen and the art of motorcycle maintenance : Robert M. Pirsig

Dream / Astral Voyaging

The Astral World : Swami Panchadasi

Appendix A: Chakra System Healing

Imagine that all of your emotional and subconscious blockages are restricted by an unbalanced chakra system. We will focus on the seven energy portals that run from the base of your spine to the crown of your head.

Get into deep meditate states through breathwork exercises, and use the power of the breathe, chi, your vital life-force to activate your self healing powers. Focus your intentions on specific chakra points, allowing your mind to release and unblock the below outlined negative attachments.

It does take time to learn how to do this, think of it as a gym workout, your strength of mind and meditation will increase with practise, patience and devotion.

Follow the fundamental guide on the next page which covers seven of the chakra points to help get you get started.

Appendix A : Energy portals of the chakra system

The Seventh: Crown: Purple
Blocked by Attachments: Accept your Divinity
Surrender and Let go

The Sixth: Third Eye: Indigo
Blocked by Illusion: Realise We are one United in Nature
Do not believe in loss or gain

The Fifth: Throat: Blue
Blocked by Denial: Know yourself and Speak your Truth
Not my Will but Thine

The Fourth: Heart: Green
Blocked by Grief: Come to Acceptance
Forgive all Betrayals, Forgive yourself

The Third: Solar Plexus: Yellow
Blocked by Shame: Focus your Awareness
View the Ego impersonally

The Second: Sacral: Orange
Blocked by Guilt: Learn to Trust
Have faith in the support of invisible realms

The First: Root: Red
Blocked by Fear: Face it and find Strength to Overcome
Accept Transformation through Death

43355719R00045

Printed in Poland
by Amazon Fulfillment
Poland Sp. z o.o., Wrocław